A
Fisherman's
Cookbook

by Daniel Hernandez

CP
Corbin Publishing
Fishing and Cookbooks

ISBN: 0-9633148-2-3

For information write:

Corbin Publishing
P.O. Box 90
Montebello, CA
90640

www.sport-fishing.com

e-mail: sptfishing@aol.com

Credits

Cover Design: David Oshima
Cover Photo: Jon Yoshinaga
Cover Food Stylist: Cathi Hofstetter
Illustrations: David Oshima
Book Design: David Oshima
Project Director: Heather Trail
Lawry's Test Kitchen Manager: Vicki Gagliano
Project Editor: Karene Wells

First Edition

Printed in the U.S.A.

Acknowledgments

First, I'd like to thank everyone at Lawry's Foods, Inc. for all their help with and support of my weekly television fishing program, *Sportfishing with Dan Hernandez*. Your help has made us one of the most popular fishing programs on television. I'd also like to thank the special people who worked with me on this book. Thank you Kirk, Vicki, Cathi, Heather, Karene, and all the many assistants at Lawry's test kitchen who tested every recipe. I'd like to thank David, Jon, and Larry, my longtime friends, who have stuck with me in this and many of my other projects.

Also, thanks to all the skippers who have worked with me over the years, and the galley cooks who shared many of their favorite ways to cook fish.

Special thanks, Mom and Dad, for your love and support.

Introduction

I'm proud to say that this cookbook is not like many you have seen in the past. This one was written by a fisherman for a fisherman, and for anyone who enjoys a great fish dish. You'll find lots of fish in this book that you won't find at your local fish market. But don't worry, we've also covered all the basic fish too, like trout, tuna, catfish and halibut, just to name a few.

This book isn't just about different ways to cook fish; it's much more than that. For those of us who have braved the high seas to do battle with giant tuna, or backpacked to lakes hidden in a high mountain pass, a fish means more than just something to eat. Most of us release many more fish than we ever take home. For us, the thrill is to be outdoors, to battle with the fish in his home waters. The thrill of landing a monster-size fish, or making that perfect cast, is what we live for, not just to kill a fish. So when we decide to take a fish home, it's not done lightly. We don't take fish from a lake or stream or even the ocean without thinking about it. We are careful not to overfish our favorite spots, to leave fish for the next fisherman that may come along. So, when we do take a fish home for a meal, we want it to be the best meal we have ever had.

In this book, you'll always find that perfect recipe to celebrate your catch with. We'll show you some terrific new ways to cook your catch, and most of the recipes are quick and easy.

I hope you enjoy *A Fisherman's Cookbook.*

Dan Hernandez

Contents

Cooking
&
Fish Handling Tips

How to Buy Fish

For those days when fish don't want to bite, it's off to the fish market we go.

Here in Southern California, where I live, we are blessed with fresh seafood markets everywhere. As a rule, if you live near an ocean or large body of water you too will find a wide selection of fresh fish to pick from. So how do you know what a fresh fish looks or smells like?

First, if it smells like fish or has an ammonia smell, then it's not fresh. Fresh fish will have no smell. Whole fish should have bright clear eyes, not sunken; and red gills, never brown. The fish should feel firm and elastic; its flesh should spring back when touched. Fillets and steaks should have moist, firm flesh and, again, the flesh should not smell at all.

If you've taken the time to find fresh fish, now it's just as important to handle it well. Some of my friends transport their fish on ice from the market to their home. With fresh fish you should cook it or refrigerate it as soon as possible. Remember, the better you handle the fish, the better it's going to taste.

One last note on fresh fish. Just because you might live hundreds of miles from the ocean doesn't mean you can't find fresh fish. Check out your local seafood selections at your supermarket. You might just be surprised by the fresh fish they have and what they might be able to order for you.

Storing and Handling Fish

Fish can be rinsed under cold running water and patted dry with paper towels before storing or cooking. I prefer to wash my fish in a bowl of cool water rather than using running water because running water can damage small and delicate fish. I also feel some nutrients are lost in running water.

If you've been out fishing, you should do most of the fish cleaning out in the field. Most lakes and piers have areas just for fish cleaning. Once home you should wash the fish again. Unless you plan to cook the fish as soon as you get home, you should immediately refrigerate your catch. When leaving a lake or dock for the trip home, your fish should already be on ice, in an ice chest.

The better your fish is handled once landed, the better it will taste. Fresh fish handled correctly will taste much better than frozen fish. You can store whole fish on crushed ice in the coldest part of the refrigerator no longer than 2 days. Fish pieces should be stored in the coldest part of the refrigerator no longer than 24 hours. Frozen fish has the best flavor if used within 2 months but can be frozen up to 4 months. Thaw frozen fish in the refrigerator. Rinse and pat dry before cooking.

Do not refreeze fish that has been previously frozen.

Filleting Fish

When filleting, our goal is to end up with pieces of boneless fish,
one from each side of the fish.

1. Cut along backbone from head to tail. Take your time and make sure not to cut into the rib area.

2. Pull the flesh away as you cut lower into the fish.

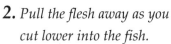

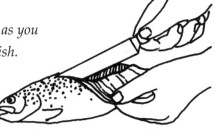

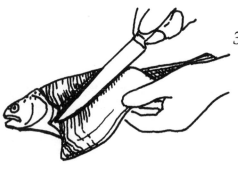

3. Now cut along the bottom of the fish to release the flesh from the fish's body.

4. Work the knife slowly between the skin and the flesh to separate the two.

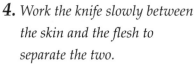

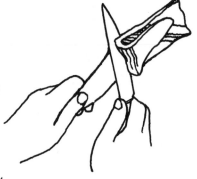

Gutting Fish

Gutting a fish is the easiest way to clean a fish.

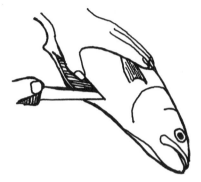

1. Your first cut should be from just below the fish's gill plate to the back hole.

2. With the fish opened up, now reach in and pull out all of the insides. You might need to use a knife.

3. Now the fish is cleaned; just run some water inside and make sure everything is out. Note that the bones are still in the fish, but it's cleaned and ready to store or cook.

Cooking Terms

Dredge: To coat lightly with flour, cornmeal or bread crumbs. It is essential that fish is dried first with a paper towel. Place coating mixture in a shallow dish. Press fish into coating, turn and repeat on the other side, completely covering all surfaces of the fish with coating.

Marinate: To soak food in a seasoned mixture. Marinating should be done in a resealable plastic bag, or a shallow glass, ceramic or stainless steel container. Refrigerate food while marinating.

Sauté: To cook food quickly in a small amount of oil over medium-high heat, stirring frequently.

Grilling Tips

Aluminum Foil Grilling: Spray foil first with nonstick cooking spray. Lay foil on grill grid and place fish directly on the foil. It is not necessary to turn fish during grilling.

Barbecue Grids: Brush with vegetable oil, or spray with non-stick cooking spray before heating grill. Use two spatulas to turn fish.

Grill Basket: Ideal for grilling whole fish or flaky fleshed fish. Spray basket with nonstick cooking spray.

Cooktimes for Grilling and Broiling

The suggested cooktimes in this book are based on a 1-inch fillet or steak. Remember, time is based on thickness, not weight.

Grilling: Grill 10 minutes per inch of thickness over medium-high heat. Fish is cooked when flesh flakes easily with a fork.

Broiling: Place broiling pan 5 inches from the heat source. Broil 8 to 10 minutes per inch of thickness; it is not necessary to turn fish during broiling. Fish is cooked when flesh flakes easily with a fork.

PACIFIC BARRACUDA

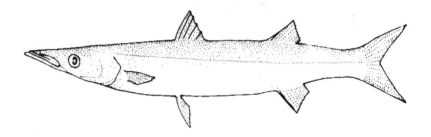

Family: Sphyraenidae (Barracudas)

Genus and Species: *Sphyraena argentea*

Common Names: Barrie, barracuda, scooter

Fat Content: Low, 11%

Protein: 74%

Yield: 40% fillet

Fish Flavor: Moderate

Range: Central California south to Magdalena Bay, Baja California, Mexico

Availability: This is available in some markets.

Barracuda Tacos

Fish tacos are THE hot new recipe. Try this one!

3/4 cup Lawry's Mesquite Marinade with Lime Juice
1 pound barracuda fillets
3/4 cup lowfat sour cream
1 1/2 tablespoons Lawry's Taco Spices & Seasonings
2 cups shredded cabbage
8 flour tortillas
Aluminum foil
Nonstick cooking spray
Salsa
Lime wedges

In resealable plastic bag, combine Mesquite Marinade with Lime Juice and fish; seal bag. Marinate in refrigerator 2 hours. Combine sour cream and Taco Spices & Seasonings; chill. Remove fish from marinade. Spray foil with nonstick cooking spray. Grill fish on aluminum foil over medium-high heat 8 to 10 minutes or until fish just begins to flake. Cut fish in bite-size pieces; spoon into warm tortillas. Top with cabbage, sour cream mixture and salsa.

Makes 4 servings (2 tacos each)

Prep time: 15 minutes   Marinate time: 2 hours
Cook time: 10 minutes

Mesquite Barracuda with Green Tomato Salsa

This recipe is a special event, but you will want to serve it often.

1 1/2 pounds barracuda, cut in 4 pieces

3/4 cup Lawry's Mesquite Marinade with Lime Juice

1 1/2 cups diced green tomatoes

1/2 cup onion, chopped

1 jalapeño chile, seeded and chopped

1 tablespoon chopped cilantro

1 teaspoon Lawry's Seasoned Salt

1/2 teaspoon Lawry's Garlic Powder with Parsley

1/2 teaspoon lime juice

1/8 teaspoon cumin

In resealable plastic bag, combine fish and Mesquite Marinade with Lime Juice; seal bag. Marinate in refrigerator 1 hour. In blender or food processor, combine remaining ingredients; blend until finely chopped. Set aside. Grill fish in a grill basket or on foil over medium-high heat 10 minutes or until fish just begins to flake. To serve, spoon salsa over grilled fish.

Makes 4 servings

HINT: Fresh tomatillos may be substituted for green tomatoes. Remove husks, rinse and quarter.

Prep time: 15 minutes   Marinate time: 1 hour
Cook time: 10 minutes

Pescado Vieja (Fish Stew)

Catch it while it's hot!

1 tablespoon vegetable oil

2 medium onions, chopped

1 green bell pepper, diced

1 package (1.5 ounces) Lawry's Original Style
   Spaghetti Sauce Spices & Seasonings

3/4 teaspoon Lawry's Garlic Powder with Parsley

1/2 teaspoon Lawry's Seasoned Salt

2 cans (14 1/2 ounces each) diced tomatoes

1 large red potato, cubed

1 can (14 1/4 ounces) beef broth

1/3 cup dry red wine

1 bay leaf

1/2 teaspoon celery seed

1 pound calico bass, sand bass or barracuda (varieties
   can be combined to equal 1 pound), cubed

In Dutch oven, heat oil over medium-high heat until hot. Add onion and bell pepper; sauté 3 minutes. Stir in remaining ingredients except fish. Bring to a boil; reduce heat, cover and simmer 20 minutes. Add fish. Simmer 10 to 15 minutes longer until fish is cooked.

Makes 10 servings

Prep time: 25 minutes
Cook time: 35 minutes

PACIFIC BONITO

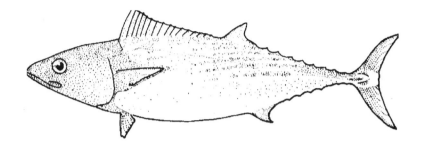

Family:	Scombridae (Mackerel and Tunas)
Genus and Species:	*Sarda chiliensis*
Common Names:	Bonehead, Laguna tuna, ocean bonito
Fat Content:	Moderate, 24%
Protein:	72%
Yield:	55% fillet
Fish Flavor:	Rich
Range:	Central California, south to Chile
Availability:	This is available in some markets.

Blackened Bonito

A combination of warm seasonings and spices.

2 1/4 teaspoons Lawry's Seasoned Salt

1 1/2 teaspoons ground black pepper

1 1/4 teaspoons Lawry's Garlic Powder with Parsley

1 teaspoon cayenne pepper

3/4 teaspoon paprika

3/4 teaspoon dried thyme leaves

3/4 teaspoon dried oregano leaves

3/4 teaspoon onion powder

1 pound bonito, cut in 1-inch-thick steaks

2 tablespoons butter, melted

1 teaspoon vegetable oil

In shallow dish, combine first 8 ingredients; blend well. Pat fish dry. Brush both sides of bonito with butter. Dredge in seasoning mixture. Heat large, heavy skillet over high heat 10 minutes. Skillet will smoke while heating. Add vegetable oil and fish to skillet. Cook 2 minutes; turn fish and cook an additional 2 minutes or until fish just begins to flake.

Makes 2 servings

Prep time: 20 minutes
Cook time: 4 minutes

Bonito with Olives and Capers

The olives, capers and tomatoes truly complement the bonito.

1 1/2 pounds bonito, cut in 4 1-inch steaks
3/4 cup Lawry's Herb & Garlic Marinade
    with Lemon Juice
1 tablespoon olive oil
1/2 cup chopped onion
1 teaspoon Lawry's Garlic Powder with Parsley
1 1/2 cups diced tomatoes
1/4 cup pimiento-stuffed green olives
1/4 cup capers

In resealable plastic bag, combine bonito and Herb & Garlic Marinade; seal bag. Marinate in refrigerator 1 hour. In medium skillet, heat oil over medium-high heat until hot. Add onion and sauté 3 minutes. Add Garlic Powder with Parsley and tomatoes; sauté 5 minutes. Place fish in baking dish; spoon onion and tomatoes over fish. Sprinkle with olives and capers. Bake in 350° F oven 15 minutes or until fish just begins to flake.

Makes 4 servings

Prep time: 15 minutes   *Marinate time: 1 hour*
Cook time: 25 minutes

Grilled Fish Fillet with Horseradish Sauce

So simple but so good!

1 bottle (12 ounces) Lawry's Herb & Garlic Marinade
    with Lemon Juice
1 to 1 1/2 pounds bonito, cut in 4 1-inch steaks
4 tablespoons butter
2 tablespoons white horseradish sauce
1 teaspoon minced fresh dill

In resealable plastic bag, combine Herb & Garlic Marinade with Lemon Juice and fish; seal bag. Marinate in refrigerator 2 hours or up to several hours. Grill over medium-high heat 3 to 5 minutes each side or until fish just begins to flake. In small saucepan, melt butter; stir in horseradish sauce. Spoon mixture over fillets and sprinkle with dill.

Makes 4 servings

HINT: If using a fish other than bonito, such as yellowtail, you may wish to sprinkle each fillet with Lawry's Seasoned Salt and Lawry's Seasoned Pepper.

Prep time: 10 minutes   *Marinate time: 2 hours*
Cook time: 10 minutes

Jamaican Jerk Bonito

A combination of the warm and spicy flavors of the Caribbean.

1 cup chopped onion
1/2 cup sliced green onions, including tops
2 jalapeño chiles, seeded
2 teaspoons fresh thyme leaves
2 teaspoons Lawry's Seasoned Salt
1/2 teaspoon Lawry's Seasoned Pepper
1/2 teaspoon Lawry's Garlic Powder with Parsley
1/2 teaspoon ground allspice
1/4 teaspoon ground cumin
1/4 teaspoon nutmeg
1 to 1 1/2 pounds bonito, cut in 4 1-inch-thick steaks
Summer Vegetable and Fruit Salsa *(see page 104)*

In food processor or blender, combine all ingredients except bonito and salsa; blend until finely chopped. Pat fish dry, rub both sides of fish with seasonings. Grill fish on foil over medium-high heat 10 minutes or until fish just begins to flake. Spoon salsa over fish and serve.

Makes 4 servings

Prep Time: 10 minutes
Cook Time: 10 minutes

CALICO BASS

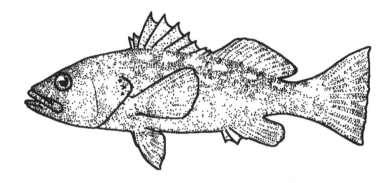

Family:	Serranidae (Sea Basses)
Genus and Species:	*Paralabrax clathratus*
Common Names:	Kelp bass, bull bass, cabrilla
Fat Content:	Low, 5%
Protein:	90%
Yield:	35-45% fillet, depending on fish size
Fish Flavor:	Mild
Range:	Central California to Magdalena Bay, Baja California, Mexico
Availability:	This is not available in markets.

Calico Bass Beignets

Beignet is French for fritter; these savory beignets make great appetizers.

1 cup calico bass, cooked and boned
1/4 cup Monterey Jack cheese, shredded
1/4 cup green onions
1 1/4 teaspoons Lawry's Seasoned Salt
1/4 teaspoon Lawry's Garlic Powder with Parsley
1/4 teaspoon cayenne pepper
1 cup fish stock
6 tablespoons butter
1 cup flour
4 eggs
2 pounds vegetable shortening for frying
Cajun Rémoulade Sauce *(see page 92)*

In small bowl, combine first 6 ingredients; blend well. In medium saucepan, combine stock and butter; bring to a boil. Reduce heat to low. With a wooden spoon, stir in flour. Continue stirring until mixture forms a ball and pulls away from the sides of the saucepan. Remove from heat. Add one egg at a time, beating well after each addition. Mixture should be smooth and glossy. Add fish mixture to flour mixture; blend well. In large skillet, heat shortening to 365°F. Drop beignet mixture by rounded teaspoonfuls. Cook until golden brown. Drain on paper towels and serve hot. Serve with Cajun Rémoulade Sauce.

Makes 24 appetizers

VARIATION: SOUTHWEST BEIGNETS
Substitute: 1/4 cup Cheddar cheese for Monterey Jack; 1/4 cup diced green chiles for green onions. Reduce Lawry's Seasoned Salt to 1 teaspoon.
Prep time: 25 minutes
Cook time: 24 minutes

Calico Bass Fillets with Tomatoes and Mushrooms

Just a few ingredients, but this is a delicious way to prepare fish.

1/2 cup Lawry's Herb & Garlic Marinade with
   Lemon Juice, divided
1/2 pound calico bass, cut in 2 pieces
1 medium tomato, diced
1/4 cup sliced mushrooms
1/4 cup sliced green onions
1/4 teaspoon Lawry's Seasoned Salt
Aluminum foil

In small bowl, place 2 tablespoons Herb & Garlic Marinade with Lemon Juice; set aside. Pour remaining marinade into resealable plastic bag; add fish and seal bag. Marinate in refrigerator 2 hours. Combine 2 tablespoons Herb & Garlic Marinade with Lemon Juice, tomato, mushrooms, green onions and Seasoned Salt; blend well. Place tomato mixture on large rectangle of aluminum foil and wrap tightly. Remove fish from marinade and grill over medium-high heat 4 to 6 minutes each side or until fish just begins to flake. Place foil pouch on grill for last 5 minutes of fish cook time. Serve heated vegetables over fish.

Makes 2 servings

Prep time: 15 minutes   *Marinate time: 2 hours*
Cook time: 12 minutes

Easy Fish Gumbo

This is stick-to-the-ribs fare, good anytime, but most appreciated when it's cold outside and you want to get warm inside. Use any kind of fish.

3 tablespoons olive oil

3/4 cup green bell pepper, diced

1 clove garlic, finely chopped

3/4 cup celery, diced

3/4 cup onion, diced

3 beef bouillon cubes

3 cups boiling water

1 can (1 pound) tomatoes, drained, juice reserved

2 cups sliced okra

1 bay leaf

2 1/2 tablespoons Lawry's Seasoned Salt

1/2 teaspoon Lawry's Seasoned Pepper

1/2 teaspoon thyme

1 1/2 pounds barracuda, calico bass or sand bass
(varieties can be combined to equal 1 1/2 pounds)

Filé seasoning (optional)

Hot pepper sauce

2 cups cooked white rice

(continued on next page)

In large skillet, heat olive oil over medium-high heat until hot. Add green bell pepper, garlic, celery and onion. Sauté 3 minutes; set aside. In large pot, dissolve bouillon cubes in boiling water and add sautéed vegetables, tomatoes, okra, bay leaf and seasonings. Cover and simmer 30 minutes. Add fish and simmer an additional 20 minutes; use tomato juice to thin if desired. Sprinkle with filé or hot sauce to taste, remove bay leaf and serve in bowls over cooked rice.

Makes 8 servings

HINT: Filé seasoning can be found in most spice sections of local grocery stores. If unable to locate, use a Cajun or gumbo seasoning.

Prep time: 30 minutes
Cook time: 50 minutes

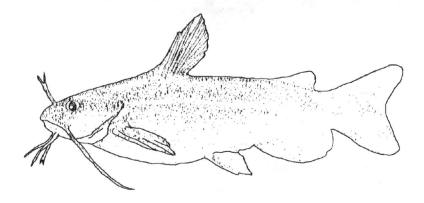

Family:	Ictaluridae (Catfishes)
Genus and Species:	*Ictalurus punctatus*
Common Names:	Channel
Fat Content:	High, 29%
Protein:	68%
Yield:	55% fillet
Fish Flavor:	Mild
Range:	Southern California, east to southern states
Availability:	This is available in most markets.

California Catfish Salad

A refreshing salad for a hot summer day.

1 pound catfish fillets, cooked and cut in bite-size
  pieces
2 medium tomatoes, coarsely chopped
1 avocado, cubed
1/3 cup chopped green onions
1/4 cup pitted and sliced green olives
1/2 cup Lawry's Classic White Wine Vinaigrette with
  Chardonnay
7 cups torn lettuce

In medium bowl, combine fish, tomatoes, avocado, onions and olives. Add White Wine Vinaigrette with Chardonnay; toss. Chill 1 hour. Remove from refrigerator and toss with lettuce.

Makes 4 servings

Prep time: 20 minutes
Chill time: 1 hour

Lemon Catfish Bake

Lemon and dill, the perfect flavor for fish fillets.

1 1/2 pounds catfish fillets, cut in 4 pieces
3/4 cup Lawry's Lemon Pepper Marinade
    with Lemon Juice
1/4 cup dry bread crumbs
1 tablespoon Lawry's Seasoned Salt
1 teaspoon Lawry's Lemon Pepper
1/2 teaspoon dried dill
Paprika
4 lemon slices (garnish)

In resealable plastic bag, combine catfish fillets and Lemon Pepper Marinade with Lemon Juice; seal bag. Marinate 1 hour in refrigerator. In pie plate, combine bread crumbs, Seasoned Salt, Lemon Pepper and dill. Remove fish from marinade; shake off excess liquid. Dredge fish in bread crumb mixture. Place in greased 12x8x2-inch baking dish. Sprinkle lightly with paprika. Bake, uncovered, in 350°F oven 25 to 30 minutes or until fish just begins to flake.

Makes 4 servings

HINT: Any type of fish fillets may be substituted.

Prep time: 10 minutes   Marinate time: 1 hour
Cook time: 30 minutes

Sautéed Catfish
with Walnut Coating

A breading that is something different, something special.

2/3 cup finely chopped walnuts

1/3 cup fine, dry bread crumbs

1 tablespoon chopped parsley

1 tablespoon Lawry's Seasoned Salt

1 teaspoon Lawry's Lemon Pepper

1 to 1 1/2 pounds catfish fillets, cut in 4 pieces

1 egg, beaten

2 tablespoons vegetable oil

In shallow baking dish, combine walnuts, bread crumbs, parsley, Seasoned Salt and Lemon Pepper. Pat fillets dry. In another shallow dish, add egg. Dip fillets in egg, then dredge in walnut mixture. In large skillet, heat oil over medium heat until hot. Cook 2 fillets at a time until golden brown on both sides, about 5 minutes each side, or until fish just begins to flake. Remove to warm platter. Repeat with remaining fillets, adding oil if necessary.

Makes 4 servings

VARIATION: Replace walnuts with finely chopped pecans.

Prep time: 20 minutes
Cook time: 20 minutes

Southern-Style Catfish

Golden and crisp outside, succulent inside.

1 1/2 pounds catfish fillets, cut in 4 pieces
1/2 cup yellow cornmeal
1 tablespoon Lawry's Seasoned Salt
1/4 teaspoon Lawry's Seasoned Pepper
1/4 teaspoon cayenne pepper
3/4 cup buttermilk
1/2 cup flour
1/3 cup vegetable oil

In shallow dish, combine cornmeal, Seasoned Salt, Seasoned Pepper and cayenne pepper. Dip fish in buttermilk, shake off excess buttermilk and dredge in flour. Dip again in buttermilk, then dredge in seasoned cornmeal. In large heavy skillet (cast iron is best), heat oil over medium-high heat until hot; fry fish about 5 minutes each side, depending on thickness, or until fish just begins to flake.

Makes 4 servings

HINT: Coat fish ahead of time; then place on tray and refrigerate until ready to fry.

Prep time: 20 minutes
Cook time: 20 minutes

Spanish-Style Baked Catfish

A colorful, authentic Spanish dish.

1 1/2 pounds catfish fillets, cut in 6 pieces

1/2 cup cornmeal

Paprika

1 medium onion, chopped

1 tablespoon olive oil

1 cup chunky salsa

1/4 cup sliced ripe olives

1 teaspoon Lawry's Garlic Salt

1 teaspoon freshly grated lemon peel

Chopped parsley (garnish)

Lemon wedges (garnish)

Pat fish dry. Dredge fish in cornmeal. Place in lightly greased 12x8x2-inch baking dish. Sprinkle with paprika. Bake in 425°F oven 20 to 25 minutes or until fish just begins to flake. Meanwhile, in medium skillet heat olive oil over medium-high heat until hot. Add onion; sauté 3 minutes. Stir in salsa, olives, Garlic Salt and lemon peel; heat through. Serve over baked fish. Garnish with parsley and lemon wedges.

Makes 6 servings

HINT: Seasoned dry bread crumbs can replace cornmeal.

Prep time: 20 minutes
Cook time: 25 minutes

HALIBUT

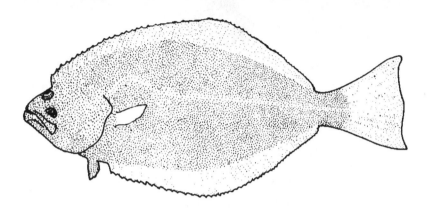

Family:	Bothidae (Left-eyed flounders)
Genus and Species:	*Paralichthys californicus*
Common Names:	Flatty, pop tart (small), barn door (large), Monterey halibut, chicken halibut, southern halibut
Fat Content:	Low, 11%
Protein:	84%
Yield:	65% fillet
Fish Flavor:	Moderate
Range:	Baja Mexico to Central California
Availability:	This can be found in most markets.

Grilled Halibut Caribbean

A sweet and savory flavor makes this sauce for grilled fish a winner.

3 tablespoons olive oil, divided
1/4 cup chopped shallots
1/3 cup chopped green bell pepper
1/3 cup chopped red bell pepper
3/4 cup chunky salsa
1/4 cup apricot preserves
1 1/2 tablespoons chopped cilantro
3/4 teaspoon Lawry's Garlic Salt
4 halibut steaks, 1-inch thick
Lawry's Seasoned Salt

In large skillet, heat 1 tablespoon olive oil over medium-high heat until hot. Add shallots and bell pepper; sauté 3 minutes. Add chunky salsa, apricot preserves, cilantro and Garlic Salt; blend well. Cook 2 minutes. Brush halibut steaks with olive oil. Sprinkle with Seasoned Salt. Grill or broil 5 minutes on each side or until fish just begins to flake. Spoon sauce over grilled fish before serving.

Makes 4 servings

Prep time: 15 minutes
Cook time: 20 minutes

Halibut Chowder

A restaurant-quality chowder.

2 tablespoons butter

1 cup chopped onion

1 carrot, chopped

1 stalk celery, chopped

1 red bell pepper, chopped

6 cups fish stock OR chicken stock

4 boiling potatoes, diced

1 medium tomato, chopped

1 bay leaf

2 tablespoons minced fresh basil

1 teaspoon Lawry's Seasoned Salt

1/2 teaspoon Lawry's Garlic Powder with Parsley

1/4 teaspoon Lawry's Seasoned Pepper

2 pounds halibut, cut in 1-inch chunks

1 cup heavy cream

In large saucepan, melt butter over medium heat. Add onion, carrot, celery and red bell pepper. Sauté 4 minutes. Add fish stock, tomato, potatoes, bay leaf, basil, Seasoned Salt, Garlic Powder with Parsley and Seasoned Pepper. Bring to a boil. Reduce heat and simmer, covered, 20 minutes. Add halibut and cook 5 minutes; stir in cream.

Makes 6 servings

HINT: Butter will separate and float on the top of chowder. Be sure to stir before serving.

Prep time: 25 minutes
Cook time: 30 minutes

Halibut Kabobs

Kabobs are popular and easy to make ahead for busy weeknight dinners.

1 pound halibut steaks, cut in 1-inch cubes
1 cup Lawry's Herb & Garlic Marinade with
    Lemon Juice, divided
4 mushroom caps
1 green bell pepper, cut in 1-inch squares
12 cherry tomatoes
4 skewers, soaked in water 1 hour

In resealable plastic bag, combine halibut and 3/4 cup Herb & Garlic Marinade with Lemon Juice; seal bag. Marinate in refrigerator 1 hour. Remove from marinade. On skewers alternate fish, green pepper, tomato and end with mushroom. Grill kabobs over medium heat 8 to 10 minutes, turning and basting frequently with reserved marinade, or until fish just begins to flake.

Makes 4 servings

Prep time: 10 minutes   *Marinate time: 1 hour*
Cook time: 10 minutes

Halibut with
Red Pepper Sauce

Herb & Garlic Marinade gives halibut just the right flavor boost.

> 1 to 1 1/2 pounds halibut fillets, cut in 4 1-inch steaks
> 1 cup Lawry's Herb & Garlic Marinade
>   with Lemon Juice
> Red Pepper Sauce *(see page 101)*

In resealable plastic bag, combine halibut and Herb & Garlic Marinade; seal bag. Marinate in refrigerator 1 hour. Grill halibut 5 minutes each side or until fish just begins to flake. Remove from grill and top with Red Pepper Sauce.

Makes 4 servings

Prep time: 5 minutes   Marinate time: 1 hour
Cook time: 10 minutes

KING SALMON

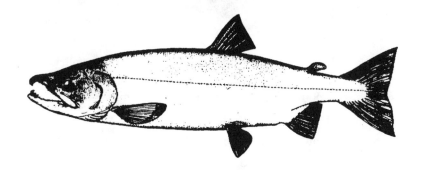

Family: Salmonidae (Salmons)

Genus and Species: *Oncorhynchus tshawytscha*

Common Names: Spring salmon, black mouth

Fat Content: High, 57%

Protein: 42%

Yield: 60-70% fillet or steak

Fish Flavor: Rich

Range: San Diego, California, to the Bering Sea and Japan

Availability: This is available in most markets.

Grilled Salmon Burgers

These are the best!

1 pound fresh skinless, boneless salmon
2 tablespoons sliced green onions
2 tablespoons Lawry's Citrus Grill Marinade with
    Orange Juice
1 teaspoon Lawry's Garlic Pepper
1/2 teaspoon Lawry's Seasoned Salt
4 hamburger buns

Place all ingredients into food processor. Process until salmon is well minced. Place mixture in medium bowl; blend well. Form into 4 patties. Grill or broil, using medium-high heat, 3 to 4 minutes on each side, or until fish just begins to flake. Serve on warm toasted hamburger buns with condiments.

Makes 4 servings

Prep time: 15 minutes
Cook time: 8 minutes

Herb-Crusted Salmon

A wonderful combination of crusty texture and light, flaky salmon.

1 1/2 pounds salmon fillets, cut in 4 1-inch pieces
1/2 cup flour
1 egg
2 tablespoons water
1/4 cup bread crumbs
1/4 cup finely chopped parsley
1/4 cup finely chopped green onions
1/4 cup finely chopped fresh dill
1 1/2 teaspoons Lawry's Seasoned Salt
1 teaspoon Lawry's Garlic Powder with Parsley
2 tablespoons olive oil

Dredge salmon in flour. In shallow dish, blend egg and water; set aside. In another shallow dish, combine bread crumbs, parsley, green onions, dill, Seasoned Salt and Garlic Powder with Parsley; blend well. Coat salmon in egg, then dredge in bread crumb mixture. In large skillet, heat oil over medium heat; add salmon and cook 3 to 5 minutes each side or until fish just begins to flake. Bread coating should be lightly browned.

Makes 4 servings

Prep time: 25 minutes
Cook time: 20 minutes

Poached Salmon Steaks

Poached salmon is an elegant dish; microwaving makes it foolproof.

1/3 cup chopped onion
1/3 cup chopped carrots
1/3 cup chopped celery
2 tablespoons butter
1 quart water
1/2 cup dry white wine
1 teaspoon Lawry's Seasoned Salt
1 teaspoon Lawry's Lemon Pepper
6 black peppercorns
1 to 1 1/2 pounds salmon steaks
Cheesecloth
Cucumber Sauce *(see page 95)*

In 3-quart glass casserole dish, combine all ingredients, except salmon. Cover and microwave on HIGH 8 minutes. Wrap salmon in cheesecloth and place in hot liquid. Cover and microwave on HIGH 4 to 5 minutes or until fish just begins to flake. Let fish stand in poaching liquid, covered, 3 minutes. Carefully remove from hot liquid and gently remove cheese-cloth. Peel off any remaining skin before serving. Liquid may be used for fish soup or stew. Serve hot or cold salmon with Cucumber Sauce.

Makes 4 servings

(continued on next page)

Stove Top Directions:

In Dutch oven or large saucepan with lid, combine all ingredients, except salmon. Cover and bring to a boil. Wrap salmon in cheesecloth and place in boiling liquid. Cover and reduce heat to low; simmer 10 to 12 minutes or until fish just begins to flake. To serve, continue with previous instructions.

Prep time: 20 minutes
Cook time: 16 minutes

Teriyaki Salmon Steaks

A convenient way to serve salmon.

1/3 cup Lawry's Teriyaki Marinade with
    Pineapple Juice
1/4 cup sherry wine
2 tablespoons orange juice
1 tablespoon Dijon mustard
1 1/2 pounds salmon, cut in 4 1-inch steaks
1 large tomato, diced
1/2 cup thinly sliced green onions

In medium bowl, blend together Teriyaki Marinade with Pineapple Juice, wine, orange juice and mustard with wire whisk; reserve 3 tablespoons for grilling. In resealable plastic bag, combine salmon and marinade mixture; seal bag. Marinate in refrigerator 1 hour. In small bowl, combine tomato and green onion; set aside. Remove salmon from marinade. Grill or broil salmon over medium-high heat, 3 to 5 minutes, brushing once with reserved marinade. Turn salmon over. Spoon vegetables over salmon; cook 3 to 5 minutes longer or until fish just begins to flake.

Makes 4 servings

Prep time: 15 minutes   *Marinate time: 1 hour*
Cook time: 10 minutes

MAKO SHARK

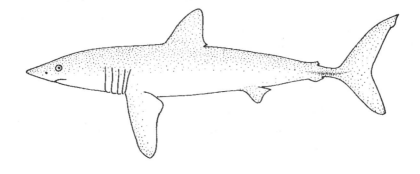

Family:	Lamnidae (Mackerel shark)
Genus and Species:	*Isurus oxyrinchus*
Common Names:	Bonito shark, mackerel shark
Fat Content:	Moderate, 12%
Protein:	81%
Yield:	80-90% steaked, depending on size of fish
Fish Flavor:	Rich
Range:	Washington to Chile
Availability:	This is available in most markets.

Citrus Grilled Baja Shark

Baja is known for its plentiful supply of fresh fish.

1 pound mako shark, cut in 2 1-inch steaks
1 cup Lawry's Citrus Marinade with Orange Juice
1/4 cup chopped onion
1 tablespoon olive oil
1 1/2 cups diced tomatoes
1 teaspoon dried basil, finely crushed
1/2 teaspoon Lawry's Seasoned Salt
1/4 teaspoon Lawry's Seasoned Pepper
1/4 teaspoon Lawry's Garlic Powder with Parsley
Fresh lemon (optional)
Fresh cilantro (garnish)

In resealable plastic bag, combine fish and Citrus Marinade with Orange Juice; seal bag. Marinate 1 hour in refrigerator. In large skillet, heat oil over medium-high heat until hot. Add onion; sauté 3 minutes. Add remaining ingredients except lemon. Bring to a boil; reduce heat, cover and simmer 15 minutes, stirring occasionally. Uncover and continue simmering 10 minutes. Remove fish from marinade. Grill fish over medium-high heat 5 minutes each side or until fish just begins to flake. Squeeze fresh lemon juice over fish while grilling, if desired. Serve sauce over fish. Garnish with cilantro.

Makes 2 servings

Prep time: 15 minutes   *Marinate time: 1 hour*
Cook time: 30 minutes

Grilled Mako Shark
with Garlic-Basil Butter

The freshness of basil and garlic butter brings incredible flavor to grilled fish.

1/2 cup soft butter
1/4 cup chopped fresh basil
1 teaspoon Lawry's Garlic Powder with Parsley
3/4 teaspoon Lawry's Seasoned Pepper
2 pounds mako shark, cut in 6 1-inch steaks
Lemon juice
Lawry's Seasoned Salt, to taste

In medium bowl, combine butter, basil, Garlic Powder with Parsley and Seasoned Pepper. Beat until smooth with electric mixer or by hand. Form butter mixture into special butter molds, or spread 1/2-inch thick on a waxed-paper-lined baking tray; refrigerate until firm. Once firm, remove butter from molds or cut butter sheet into 1-inch square pads. Refrigerate until needed. Brush fish steaks with lemon juice and sprinkle with Seasoned Salt. Grill 5 minutes on each side over medium-high heat or until fish just begins to flake. Top fish with flavored butter. Serve immediately.

Makes 6 servings

Prep time: 10 minutes   *Chill Time: 1 hour*
Cook time: 10 minutes

Prize Catch Mako Shark

Traditional Mediterranean flavors combine to deliver on taste.

1 tomato, chopped
1 cup sliced fresh mushrooms
1 small red onion, diced
1 green bell pepper, diced
1 1/2 pounds mako shark, cut in 4 1-inch steaks
Olive oil
Lawry's Garlic Salt, to taste
Lawry's Seasoned Pepper, to taste
4 pieces of 12x8-inch parchment paper or foil
4 ounces feta cheese, crumbled (garnish)

In medium bowl, combine tomato, mushrooms, onion and bell pepper. Brush both sides of fish with olive oil, and season with Garlic Salt and Seasoned Pepper. Fold each piece of paper lengthwise in half. Place fish on one side of fold for each piece of paper. Spoon vegetables evenly over fish. Fold other side of each paper over fish; crimp edges together to seal securely. Place on cookie sheet. Bake in 350°F oven 13 to 20 minutes depending on fish thickness. Transfer packets to individual serving plates and open right before eating. Sprinkle with feta cheese.

Makes 4 servings
HINT: Each packet (using parchment paper) may be microwaved on HIGH 6 to 8 minutes, rotating half a turn each 2 minutes.

Prep time: 20 minutes
Cook time: 20 minutes

Yucatan Mako Shark

A mixture of sweet fruits and citrus gives this dish an exciting flavor.

1/2 cup orange juice
1/4 cup lime juice
1/4 cup soy sauce
1/2 teaspoon Lawry's Garlic Powder with Parsley
1 to 1 1/2 pounds mako shark, cut in 4 1-inch steaks
1/2 cup chopped onion
1/2 cup diced red bell pepper
1 tablespoon vegetable oil
1 cup diced fresh papaya OR mango
2/3 cup diced orange segments
2 teaspoons finely diced jalapeño chile, seeded
    and chopped
1 tablespoon lime juice
1 teaspoon finely chopped cilantro
Orange slices (garnish)
Fresh cilantro (garnish)

In small bowl, combine first four ingredients. In resealable plastic bag, combine 1/2 cup orange juice mixture and fish; seal bag. Refrigerate 1 to 6 hours. In large skillet, heat oil over medium-high heat until hot. Add onion and bell pepper; sauté 3 minutes. Add remaining orange juice mixture, papaya, oranges, jalapeño, lime juice and cilantro; simmer 5 to 7 minutes. Remove fish from orange mixture. Grill over medium-high heat 5 minutes each side or until fish just begins to flake. To serve, arrange fish fillets on plate. Top with papaya citrus salsa. Garnish with orange slices and cilantro.

Makes 4 servings

Prep time: 25 minutes   Marinate time: 1 hour
Cook time: 20 minutes

RAINBOW TROUT

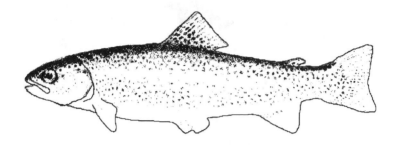

Family: Salmonidae (Trouts and Chars)

Genus and Species: *Salmo gairdneri*

Common Names: Steelhead trout

Fat Content: High, 54%

Protein: 45%

Yield: 70% fillet

Fish Flavor: Mild

Range: United States, especially in the West

Availability: This is available in most markets, but sport-caught, holdover trout taste much better than farm raised.

Grilled Whole Trout

You may substitute your favorite whole fish.

4 small whole trout
Lawry's Seasoned Salt
2 lemons, sliced
4 sprigs fresh basil
4 green onions
Olive oil
Creole Butter Sauce *(see page 94)*

Sprinkle inside and outside of trout with Seasoned Salt; let stand 10 to 15 minutes. Place several lemon slices, basil and green onion securely inside of trout; brush outside generously with olive oil. Grill trout in grill basket over medium-high heat 5 minutes on each side or until fish just begins to flake. Serve warm Creole Butter Sauce over trout.

Makes 4 servings

Prep time: 25 minutes
Cook time: 10 minutes

Planked Trout

Cooking the fish on a wood plank imparts delicious flavor and aroma.

2 whole trout
3 tablespoons olive oil
Lawry's Seasoned Salt, to taste
Lawry's Lemon Pepper, to taste
1 hardwood plank, 12 inches x 12 inches, 1-inch thick

Brush skin of trout with olive oil. Sprinkle Seasoned Salt and Lemon Pepper inside the cavity and on the skin of the trout. Brush plank with olive oil. Place plank in cold oven; heat at 350°F for 15 minutes. Remove plank from oven; place fish, skin-side down on plank. Bake in 350°F oven 25 minutes.

Use hardwoods such as cedar, alder, hickory, maple or oak. Avoid resinous woods like pine. Plank should be clean and unvarnished.

For a dramatic presentation, serve fish on plank at the table.

Makes 2 servings

HINT: The plank cooking method maybe used for fillets and whole fish of many varieties.

Prep time: 20 minutes
Cook time: 25 minutes

Stuffed Trout

A great recipe when the fisherman wants to show off that great catch!

4 whole trout (about 2 pounds)
1 bottle (12 ounces) Lawry's Lemon Pepper Marinade
   with Lemon Juice
1 tablespoon butter
1/4 cup chopped onion
1/4 cup chopped celery
2 cups seasoned stuffing mix
3 tablespoons fish stock OR chicken stock
1/2 teaspoon Lawry's Lemon Pepper

Pierce skin of trout with fork. In resealable plastic bag, combine fish and Lemon Pepper Marinade with Lemon Juice; seal bag. Marinate in refrigerator 2 hours. In medium skillet, melt butter over medium-high heat. Add onion and celery; sauté 3 minutes. Add remaining ingredients; blend well. Spoon dressing into trout. Bake in 350° F oven 15 minutes or until fish just begins to flake.

Makes 4 servings

Prep time: 10 minutes   *Marinate time: 2 hours*
Cook time: 20 minutes

Teriyaki Trout

Easy and quick.

4 whole trout (about 2 pounds)
3/4 cup Lawry's Teriyaki Marinade
    with Pineapple Juice
1/2 cup sliced green onions
2 medium lemons, sliced
Chopped fresh parsley (garnish)

Pierce skin of trout with fork several times. Place trout in shallow baking pan. Brush the inside and outside of each trout with Teriyaki Marinade with Pineapple Juice. Stuff with green onions and lemon slices; cover. Refrigerate 30 minutes. Place trout in oiled grill basket; brush with marinade. Grill over medium-high heat 5 minutes each side or until fish just begins to flake. Sprinkle with parsley if desired.

Makes 4 servings

Prep time: 10 minutes   *Marinate time: 30 minutes*
Cook time: 10 minutes

Trout Amandine

A classic.

2 whole trout
Lawry's Seasoned Salt, to taste
Lawry's Seasoned Pepper, to taste
Flour
3 tablespoons butter
1/2 cup sliced almonds
Parsley (garnish)
Lemon slices (garnish)

Sprinkle cavity of trout with Seasoned Salt and Seasoned Pepper. Dredge trout in flour. In large skillet, melt butter over medium-high heat. Add trout and almonds; sauté 3 to 5 minutes each side. Stir almonds frequently to brown. Cook trout until it just begins to flake. Remove fish to platter; spoon almonds over fish. Garnish with parsley and lemon slices.

Makes 2 servings

Prep time: 15 minutes
Cook time: 10 minutes

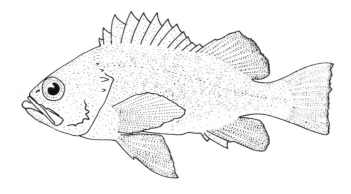

Family:	Scorpaenidae (Scorpionfishes)
Genus and Species:	*Sebastes miniatus*
Common Names:	Vermilion rockfish, red rock cod
Fat Content:	Low, 9%
Protein:	88%
Yield:	35% fillet
Fish Flavor:	Mild
Range:	California south to Northern Baja California, Mexico
Availability:	This is available in most markets.

Fish Balls Tunisian

An excellent appetizer for using pieces of fish.

1 1/2 pounds red snapper, bones removed
1 1/2 cups fresh bread crumbs
1/4 cup chopped parsley
2 onions, finely chopped
1 1/2 teaspoons Lawry's Seasoned Salt
3/4 teaspoon Lawry's Garlic Powder with Parsley
1/8 teaspoon cayenne pepper
1 egg
Oil for frying
Cocktail Sauce *(see page 93)*

In food processor, combine all ingredients, except egg and oil. Process until all ingredients are blended. Add egg; mix until egg is incorporated. Form mixture into 1-inch balls. In large skillet, pour oil to a depth of 2 inches; heat over medium heat. Add fish balls to fry, about 6 minutes per batch, turning frequently to brown. Serve with Cocktail Sauce.

Makes 24 fish balls

HINT: For a lower fat version, bake fish balls in 350°F oven 15 to 20 minutes. Spray with cooking spray to brown and crisp.

Prep time: 30 minutes
Cook time: 25 minutes

Red Snapper a la Vera Cruz

Olives, chiles and tomatoes are flavorful with fish.

1 to 1 1/2 pounds red snapper fillets, cut in 4 pieces
Lemon juice
Lawry's Seasoned Salt, to taste
Lawry's Seasoned Pepper, to taste
5 tablespoons olive oil, divided
1/2 cup chopped onion
1/2 teaspoon Lawry's Garlic Powder with Parsley
1 1/2 cups diced tomatoes
1 bay leaf
1/4 cup sliced pimiento-stuffed green olives
2 tablespoons chopped green chiles

Rub both sides of fish with lemon juice; sprinkle with Seasoned Salt and Seasoned Pepper. In large skillet, heat 3 tablespoons olive oil over medium-high heat until hot; gently cook fish, 1 minute on each side. Remove to baking dish. In same skillet, add onion and Garlic Powder with Parsley; sauté 3 minutes. Add tomatoes, bay leaf and Seasoned Pepper to taste. Bring to a boil. Reduce heat to low; simmer, uncovered, 15 to 20 minutes, stirring occasionally. Top fish with olives and chiles. Remove bay leaf from sauce; pour sauce over fish. Drizzle with olive oil. Bake, uncovered, in 300°F oven 30 minutes or until fish just begins to flake.

Makes 4 servings
Prep time: 20 minutes
Cook time: 30 minutes

Red Snapper Quesadillas

Quesadillas are a great snack or light lunch.

8 ounces red snapper fillets
1/2 cup Lawry's Citrus Grill Marinade
    with Orange Juice
1/2 cup Monterey Jack cheese, shredded
1/2 cup Cheddar cheese, shredded
1/4 cup green onions, chopped
8 flour tortillas
2 tablespoons vegetable oil
Fresh Avocado Mango Pineapple Salsa *(see page 97)*

In resealable plastic bag, combine red snapper and Lawry's Citrus Grill Marinade with Orange Juice; seal bag. Marinate in refrigerator 1 hour. Grill fish over medium-high heat 5 minutes each side or until fish just begins to flake. Cut into bite-size pieces, bones removed. Divide equally onto flour tortillas. Sprinkle with Monterey Jack cheese, Cheddar cheese and green onions. Top with flour tortilla. In large skillet, over medium-high heat, heat 1 teaspoon vegetable oil for each quesadilla. Cook both sides until lightly browned. Serve with fresh Avocado Mango Pineapple Salsa.

Makes 4 servings

Prep time: 15 minutes   Marinate time: 1 hour
Cook time: 20 minutes

SAND BASS

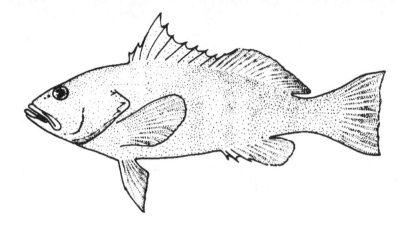

Family:	Serranidae (Sea Basses)
Genus and Species:	*Paralabrax nebulifer*
Common Names:	Barred bass, sandy, rock bass
Fat Content:	Low, 6%
Protein:	89%
Yield:	35-45% fillet, depends on fish size
Fish Flavor:	Mild
Range:	Santa Cruz, California, to Magdalena Bay, Baja California, Mexico
Availability:	This is not available in markets.

Fish & Chips

An old English favorite made American-style.

1 pound sand bass fillets, cut in
    2-inch x 1 1/2-inch strips
Lawry's Lemon Pepper
Vegetable oil for frying
2/3 cup all-purpose flour
2 teaspoons Lawry's Seasoned Salt
2/3 cup water
1 tablespoon malt vinegar
1/2 teaspoon baking soda
Prepared French fries

Pat fillets dry and sprinkle fish with Lemon Pepper on both
sides; set aside. Pour oil 3 inches deep into fryer; heat to 375°F.
In medium bowl, combine flour and Seasoned Salt; set aside.
In small bowl, combine water, vinegar and baking soda. Stir
vinegar mixture into flour mixture; beat until smooth. Dip fish
into batter; allow excess batter to drip into bowl. Fry 4 pieces
at a time until medium brown, turning once. Drain on paper
towels. Serve immediately with French fries.

Makes 4 servings

Prep time: 15 minutes
Cook time: 12 minutes

Lemon Pepper Grill

Citrus flavors add excitement to fish!

1 bottle (12 ounces) Lawry's Lemon Pepper Marinade
    with Lemon Juice
1 1/2 teaspoons Lawry's Lemon Pepper
1/2 cup orange juice
1/3 cup chopped cilantro
3/4 teaspoon crushed red pepper
1 to 1 1/2 pounds sand bass fillets, cut in 4 pieces
Orange slices (garnish)
Lemon wedges (garnish)

In medium bowl, combine first five ingredients; then pour into
resealable plastic bag. Add fish, seal bag and marinate in
refrigerator 30 minutes. Grill or broil over medium-high heat
5 to 7 minutes each side or until fish just begins to flake.
Garnish with orange slices and lemon wedges.

Makes 4 servings

Prep time: 10 minutes   Marinate time: 30 minutes
Cook time: 14 minutes

Sand Bass with Lime Cilantro Sauce

The Lime Cilantro Sauce is an excellent complement to fish.

1 teaspoon Lawry's Seasoned Pepper
1 teaspoon Lawry's Garlic Powder with Parsley
3 tablespoons butter
6 tablespoons lime juice
6 tablespoons pineapple juice
2 tablespoons chopped cilantro
8 ounces sand bass fillets, skinned and cut in 2 pieces

In small bowl, combine Seasoned Pepper and Garlic Powder with Parsley; blend well. In large skillet, melt butter over medium-high heat. Add sand bass and cook over medium-high heat until brown, 3 to 5 minutes each side, or until fish just begins to flake. Sprinkle 1 teaspoon of the seasoning mixture over fish. Remove fish and set aside. In same skillet, combine remaining seasoning mixture, 3 tablespoons lime juice, 3 tablespoons pineapple juice and 1 tablespoon cilantro. Reduce pan juices over medium-high heat 2 to 4 minutes. Return fish to skillet to coat with sauce. Remove fish to serving platter. Add remaining ingredients to skillet; reduce again. Pour sauce over fish.

Makes 2 servings

Prep time: 10 minutes
Cook time: 20 minutes

SCULPIN

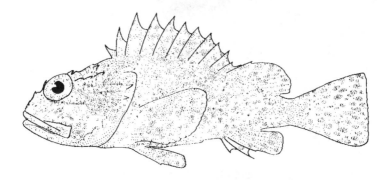

Family:	Scorpaenidae (Scorpionfishes)
Genus and Species:	*Scorpaena guttata*
Common Names:	Rattlesnake, bullhead
Fat Content:	Low, 5%
Protein:	89%
Yield:	35% fillet
Fish Flavor:	Mild, sweet
Range:	Washington to Chile
Availability:	This is not available in markets. Be very careful when handling. This is a poisonous fish; it's also a great eating fish.

Fabulous Sculpin Fillets

A delicate fish dish, flavored with mushrooms and wine.

1 teaspoon Lawry's Seasoned Salt
1/2 teaspoon Lawry's Garlic Powder with Parsley
1/2 teaspoon Lawry's Seasoned Pepper
1/2 cup flour
2 tablespoons butter OR margarine
1/2 cup dry vermouth OR dry sherry wine
1 to 1 1/2 pounds sculpin fillets, cut in 4 pieces
1/4 teaspoon chicken bouillon granules
1/4 cup water
1/4 cup minced shallots
1/2 pound fresh mushrooms, sliced
2 teaspoons minced parsley (garnish)

In 9-inch pie plate, combine Seasoned Salt, Garlic Powder with Parsley, Seasoned Pepper and flour. Dredge fish in seasoning mixture; set aside. In large skillet over medium heat, add butter; heat until butter is melted. Add wine to melted butter. Add sculpin; reduce heat to low; cover and simmer 10 minutes. Remove fish to serving platter and keep warm. In same skillet, add chicken bouillon, water, shallots and mushrooms to butter-wine liquid over medium-high heat. Sauté 3 minutes. Spoon over fish. Garnish with parsley.

Makes 4 servings

Prep time: 15 minutes
Cook time: 13 minutes

Fiesta Sculpin Fillets

Any type of fish fillets may be substituted for sculpin.

1 medium tomato, chopped

1/2 cup chopped red onion

2 tablespoons chopped green bell pepper

1/2 teaspoon Lawry's Seasoned Salt

Dash hot pepper sauce

2 tablespoons dry white wine

2 tablespoons olive oil

1 teaspoon lime juice

1/2 teaspoon Lawry's Seasoned Salt

1/4 teaspoon Lawry's Seasoned Pepper

1 1/2 pounds sculpin fillets, cut in 4 pieces

In medium bowl, combine first five ingredients; blend well and set aside. In small bowl, combine white wine, olive oil, lime juice, Seasoned Salt and Seasoned Pepper. Brush fillets with wine mixture. Place fillets on lightly greased broiler pan. Broil 7 minutes each side, basting often with wine mixture. Remove from oven and top with tomato mixture.

Makes 4 servings

Prep time: 25 minutes
Cook time: 14 minutes

Thai-Style Sculpin
with Vegetables

Cooking fish in the microwave is easy.
The Thai marinade gives this recipe a punch of spicy flavor.

1 to 1 1/2 pounds sculpin fillets, cut in 4 pieces
3/4 cup plus 1 tablespoon Lawry's Thai Ginger
    Marinade with Lime Juice
2 celery stalks, cut in thin diagonal slices
1 red bell pepper, cut in thin strips
2 cups napa cabbage leaves, torn in bite-size pieces

In resealable plastic bag, combine sculpin and 3/4 cup Thai
Ginger Marinade with Lime Juice; seal bag. Marinate in refrigerator 30 minutes. Remove fish from marinade and place in
9x12x2-inch glass baking dish. Cover with plastic wrap; vent
one corner. Microwave on HIGH 3 minutes; rotate once half-
way through cook time. Microwaving is complete when edges
of fish are firm and opaque and the center is translucent. Let
fish stand, covered, 5 minutes to finish cooking. In 2-quart
glass round baking dish, combine vegetables; cover with
plastic wrap; vent one corner. Microwave on HIGH 2 1/2
minutes. Remove from microwave; add 1 tablespoon marinade and blend well. To serve, spoon vegetables on plate and
top with fish.

Makes 4 servings

Prep time: 15 minutes   *Marinate time: 30 minutes*
Cook time: 11 minutes

SHEEPHEAD

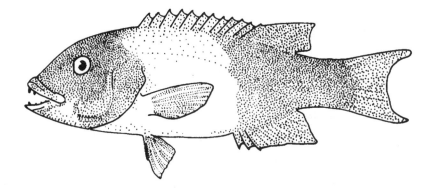

Family: Labridae (Wrasses)

Genus and Species: *Semicossyphus pulcher*

Common Names: Sheepie, goat, fathead

Fat Content: Low, 4%

Protein: 90%

Yield: 60% fillet

Fish Flavor: Mild

Range: Central California to Southern Baja California, Mexico

Availability: Not readily available, you'll have to do some looking.

Fish Fillet Sauté

A simple-to-prepare fish dish for any occasion.

1 1/2 tablespoons sweet butter
1/2 pound sheephead fillets, cut in 2 pieces
1 teaspoon Lawry's Seasoned Salt
1/2 teaspoon dried tarragon leaves, crushed
Dash paprika
2 teaspoons lemon juice
2 tablespoons diagonally sliced green onion (garnish)
Lemon wedges (garnish)

In medium skillet, melt butter over medium-high heat. Add fish and lightly brown, about 3 to 5 minutes each side or until fish just begins to flake. Sprinkle with Seasoned Salt, tarragon and paprika. Remove fish to serving platter and keep warm. In same skillet, add lemon juice; blend well with drippings. To serve, pour lemon sauce over fish; garnish with green onion and lemon wedges.

Makes 2 servings

Prep time: 10 minutes
Cook time: 15 minutes

Fish Cakes

Similar to crab cakes, but a lot less expensive.

2 eggs
2 tablespoons mayonnaise
1 teaspoon dry mustard
1 teaspoon Lawry's Seasoned Pepper
1/4 teaspoon cayenne pepper
1/8 teaspoon Lawry's Seasoned Salt
1 pound sheephead, cooked and flaked
3 tablespoons finely chopped fresh parsley
3 tablespoons crushed saltine crackers
2 tablespoons sautéed diced onion (4 tablespoons uncooked)
1 tablespoon sautéed diced celery (3 tablespoons uncooked)
Vegetable oil for frying
1/2 cup crushed saltine crackers
1/2 teaspoon Lawry's Seasoned Salt
1/4 teaspoon Lawry's Seasoned Pepper
3 eggs, beaten
Tartar Sauce *(see page 103)*

In large bowl, beat 2 eggs. Add mayonnaise, mustard, Seasoned Pepper, cayenne pepper and Seasoned Salt; blend well. Add fish, parsley and 3 tablespoons saltine crackers; blend well. Divide mixture into 8 equal patties about 2 inches in diameter. Chill 30 minutes. In deep skillet, heat oil to 365°F. In shallow dish, combine 1/2 cup saltine crackers, Seasoned Salt and Seasoned Pepper; blend well. In small bowl, beat 3 eggs for coating. Dip patties into egg, then dredge in crumb mixture. Fry 4 patties at a time until golden brown, about 3 to 5 minutes on each side. Drain cooked patties on paper towels. Serve hot with Tartar Sauce.

Makes 4 servings

Prep time: 50 minutes
Cook time: 10 minutes

Pizza

A quick, complete meal.

1 Italian 12-inch pizza shell
3 tablespoons Lawry's Classic San Francisco Dressing
    with Romano Cheese
1 medium tomato, sliced
1 medium yellow bell pepper, sliced
1 1/2 teaspoons Lawry's Garlic Salt
1/2 cup sheephead, cooked and boned
1 cup mozzarella cheese, shredded
1/4 cup Parmesan cheese, grated

Brush each side of pizza shell with 1 tablespoon Classic San
Francisco Dressing with Romano Cheese. Place on baking
sheet; broil 1 minute on each side or until lightly browned. In
medium bowl, combine tomato, yellow bell pepper, remaining
Classic San Francisco Dressing with Romano Cheese and
Garlic Salt; toss. Top pizza shell with vegetables, fish and
cheeses. Broil 8 to 10 minutes.

Makes 4 servings

Prep time: 15 minutes
Cook time: 12 minutes

Sheephead with Dill-Mustard Sauce

A lower-fat version of a classic sauce.

3 tablespoons plain nonfat yogurt

3 tablespoons mayonnaise

1 tablespoon minced fresh dill

2 teaspoons Dijon mustard

1 teaspoon chives OR green onion, minced

1 teaspoon lemon juice

1 teaspoon Lawry's Lemon Pepper

1/2 pound sheephead fillet, cut in 2 pieces

In small bowl, combine all ingredients except fish. Let stand 15 minutes or longer to blend flavors. Grill fish fillets over medium-high heat, 5 minutes each side, or until fish just begins to flake. To serve, spoon sauce over or alongside grilled fish.

Makes 2 servings

Prep time: 20 minutes
Cook time: 10 minutes

WHITE SEABASS

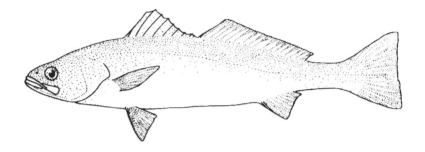

Family:	Sciaenidae (Croakers)
Genus and Species:	*Cynoscion nobilis*
Common Names:	Sea trout, weakfish, king croaker
Fat Content:	Low, 4%
Protein:	90%
Yield:	45% fillet, 70% steak
Fish Flavor:	Mild
Range:	Northern California to Central Baja California, Mexico
Availability:	This is available in most markets.

Fish Tacos

Deliciously different!

1 egg
2 tablespoons water
1 package (1 ounce) Lawry's Taco Spices & Seasonings, reserving 1 teaspoon
3 tablespoons flour
1 pound white seabass, cut in 1-inch x 4-inch pieces
Vegetable oil for frying
2 cups shredded cabbage
1/4 cup sour cream
8 corn tortillas
Salsa

In shallow dish, combine egg and water; blend well. In another shallow dish, combine Taco Spices & Seasonings (less 1
teaspoon reserved for cabbage) and flour. Pat fish dry, dip in
egg and then dredge in seasonings. In large skillet, heat oil
over medium-high heat until hot. Fry fish about 3 minutes or
until lightly browned, turning once during cooking; set aside.
In small bowl, combine sour cream and reserved Taco Spices &
Seasonings; add cabbage. Toss to blend well. Spoon fish into
warmed tortillas; top with cabbage and salsa.

Makes 4 servings

*HINT: Any firm white-flesh fish may be substituted for
seabass.*

Prep time: 15 minutes
Cook time: 6 minutes

Grilled White Seabass

Simple but tasty. This application of seasonings works well on most fish.

> 1 1/2 pounds white seabass, cut in 4 1-inch-thick
>   pieces
> 1/4 cup olive oil
> Lawry's Lemon Pepper, to taste
> Lawry's Seasoned Salt, to taste

Brush white seabass with olive oil. Sprinkle both sides of fillet with Lemon Pepper and Seasoned Salt. Grill over medium-high heat 5 minutes each side or until fish just begins to flake.

Makes 4 servings

Prep time: 5 minutes
Cook time: 10 minutes

Stuffed Mushrooms with White Seabass

A bite-size delight.

1/2 cup white seabass, cooked and boned

1/2 cup cream cheese

3 tablespoons bread crumbs

2 tablespoons chopped parsley

1/2 tablespoon Lawry's Garlic Powder with Parsley

1/4 teaspoon Lawry's Seasoned Salt

1/4 teaspoon Lawry's Seasoned Pepper

6 to 10 drops hot chile sauce, to taste

24 medium mushrooms, stems removed

3 tablespoons grated Parmesan cheese

In medium bowl, combine all ingredients except mushrooms and Parmesan cheese; blend well. Spoon mixture into mushroom caps; sprinkle with Parmesan cheese. Place stuffed mushrooms on baking sheet. Broil until lightly browned, about 3 to 5 minutes.

Makes 24 appetizers

Prep time: 15 minutes
Cook time: 5 minutes

White Seabass Lawry's Style

A delicious idea.

2 (4 ounces) white seabass fillets, 1-inch thick
1 lemon
Lawry's Seasoned Salt, to taste
Lawry's Seasoned Pepper, to taste
1 tablespoon chopped parsley
1 tablespoon melted butter

Place white seabass in baking dish. Squeeze juice of lemon over fillets. Sprinkle with Seasoned Salt, Seasoned Pepper and parsley. Pour melted butter over fillets. Place fish under broiler and cook approximately 10 to 15 minutes or until fish just begins to flake.

Makes 1 to 2 servings

Prep time: 10 minutes
Cook time: 15 minutes

YELLOWFIN TUNA

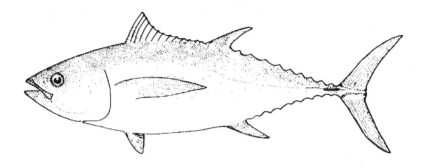

Family: Scombridea (Mackerel and Tunas)

Genus and Species: *Thunnus albacares*

Common Names: Leaping tuna, footballs, ahi, tunny

Fat Content: High, 25%

Protein: 72%

Yield: 60% fillet or steak

Fish Flavor: Rich

Range: Worldwide in all but the coldest seas

Availability: This is available in most markets.

Fettuccine and Yellowfin

This pasta dish is lovely served anytime.

3/4 pound yellowfin fillets, cut in 1-inch cubes
1/2 cup Lawry's Herb & Garlic Marinade
   with Lemon Juice
1/3 cup red bell pepper, chopped
1 tablespoon olive oil
3 tablespoons butter
3 tablespoons flour
1 1/2 cups milk
1 teaspoon Lawry's Garlic Powder with Parsley
1 teaspoon Lawry's Seasoned Salt
1/2 cup grated Parmesan cheese
8 ounces fettuccine noodles, cooked and drained

In resealable plastic bag, combine yellowfin and Herb & Garlic Marinade with Lemon Juice; seal bag. Marinate in refrigerator 1 hour. Remove fish from marinade. In large skillet, heat oil over medium-high heat. Add yellowfin and red bell pepper; sauté 3 minutes; set aside. In medium saucepan, melt butter over low heat; stir in flour. Whisk until smooth. Gradually add milk; stir with wire whisk until sauce is thickened. To sauce, add Garlic Powder with Parsley, Seasoned Salt and Parmesan cheese. Pour sauce over noodles; add yellowfin and red bell pepper, tossing to blend well. Serve immediately.

Makes 4 servings

Prep time: 10 minutes   Marinate time: 1 hour
Cook time: 30 minutes

Fish Burgers

A variety of fish may be used for this recipe. Shark and tuna are perfect.

1 pound fish fillet, boned

1/2 cup onion, finely chopped

1 egg white

1/4 cup bread crumbs

2 teaspoons Lawry's Lemon Pepper Marinade with
      Lemon Juice

1 1/2 teaspoons Lawry's Seasoned Salt

1/2 teaspoon Lawry's Seasoned Pepper

3 tablespoons vegetable oil

4 onion buns

Green leaf lettuce

1 tomato, sliced

Lemon Pepper Tarter Sauce *(see page 100)*

In food processor, process fish until shredded. Add egg white, bread crumbs, Lemon Pepper Marinade with Lemon Juice, Seasoned Salt and Seasoned Pepper. Process until well blended. Form into 4 1/2-inch-thick patties. Brush each side of patty with oil. Brush grill with oil or grill patties on foil. Grill fish patties over medium-high heat 4 to 5 minutes each side. Remove from grill and top each fish burger with Lemon Pepper Tartar Sauce, green leaf lettuce and tomato.

Makes 4 servings

Prep time: 10 minutes
Cook time: 10 minutes

Mediterranean Yellowfin Sauté

A colorful presentation of a simple meal.

2 tablespoons olive oil, divided
1 onion, chopped
4 fresh mushrooms, sliced
1 green bell pepper, sliced
1/2 teaspoon Lawry's Seasoned Salt
1/2 teaspoon Lawry's Lemon Pepper
1/4 teaspoon Lawry's Garlic Powder with Parsley
1 1/2 pounds yellowfin, cut in 4 1-inch steaks

In large skillet, heat 1 tablespoon oil over medium-high heat until hot. Add onion, mushrooms and green pepper. Sauté 3 minutes. Add Seasoned Salt, Lemon Pepper and Garlic Powder with Parsley. Transfer vegetables to bowl; keep warm. In same skillet, heat 1 tablespoon oil and cook fish over medium-high heat 5 minutes each side or until fish just begins to flake. Arrange vegetables over fish.

Makes 4 servings

HINT: Fish may be seasoned with Lawry's Lemon Pepper and Lawry's Seasoned Salt.

Prep time: 15 minutes
Cook time: 12 minutes

Teriyaki Jerky

Great for yellowfin, shark and yellowtail.

1 pound firm-fleshed fish, cut in 1/4-inch strips
3/4 cup Lawry's Teriyaki Marinade
   with Pineapple Juice

In resealable plastic bag, combine fish and Teriyaki Marinade with Pineapple Juice; seal bag. Marinate in refrigerator 1 hour. Spray a metal cooling rack with nonstick cooking spray. Place rack in a shallow baking pan. Remove fish from marinade and lay on cooling rack. Bake in oven at lowest temperature setting about 6 hours. Jerky should be dry but pliable. Cool; store in airtight container or plastic bag in refrigerator up to 2 weeks. May be frozen up to 2 months.

Makes 8 snack servings

Prep time: 1 hour
Cook time: 6 hours

Teriyaki Stir-Fry with Yellowfin

Fish brings a new twist to stir-fry.

3/4 pound yellowfin fillets, cut in thin strips
1/3 cup Lawry's Teriyaki Marinade with
    Pineapple Juice
2 tablespoons peanut oil
1 teaspoon minced fresh ginger
1/2 teaspoon Lawry's Garlic Powder with Parsley
2 cups broccoli flowerettes
2 green onions, cut in 1-inch pieces
1 large carrot, cut in 1/2-inch julienne pieces
1 tablespoon water

In resealable plastic bag, combine yellowfin and Teriyaki
Marinade with Pineapple Juice; seal bag. Marinate in refrigerator 20 minutes. In large wok or skillet, heat peanut oil over
medium-high heat until hot. Add yellowfin, ginger and Garlic
Powder with Parsley; stir-fry about 3 minutes. Add remaining
ingredients; stir-fry 5 minutes or until cooked.

Makes 4 servings

Prep time: 25 minutes   *Marinate time: 20 minutes*
Cook time: 10 minutes

Yellowfin Salad
with
Classic Caesar Dressing

A robust entrée salad.

6 cups romaine lettuce, torn in pieces
3/4 pound yellowfin, cooked and cut in 1-inch cubes
1 can (15 ounces) black olives, drained
1 can (15 ounces) garbanzo beans, drained
1 cup garlic-flavored croutons
1/4 cup Parmesan cheese, grated
2/3 cup Lawry's Classic Caesar with Imported
    Anchovies Salad Dressing
Lawry's Seasoned Salt, to taste
Lawry's Seasoned Pepper, to taste

In large bowl, combine all ingredients. Toss salad to distribute dressing.

Makes 4 servings

Prep time: 25 minutes

YELLOWTAIL

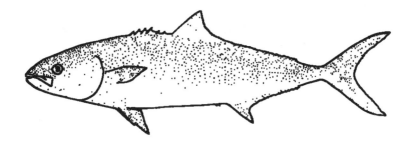

Family:	Carangidae (Jacks)
Genus and Species:	*Seriola lalandi*
Common Names:	Yellow, forktail, mossback
Fat Content:	Moderate, 12%
Protein:	80%
Yield:	60% fillet
Fish Flavor:	Moderate
Range:	Southern California south to Northern Chile
Availability:	This is available in most markets.

Salad Niçoise

The classic Niçoise with the addition of yellowtail is delightful.

> 8 ounces yellowtail fillet
> 1/2 cup Lawry's Herb & Garlic Marinade
>   with Lemon Juice
> 3 cups green leaf lettuce, torn
> 4 cups iceberg lettuce, torn
> 1/4 green bell pepper, cut in strips
> 2 hard-cooked eggs, sliced in half
> 16 pitted black olives
> 1 small onion, thinly sliced
> 1 medium tomato, cut in 8 wedges
> 1 package (9 ounces) frozen French-cut green beans,
>   cooked and drained
> 1 teaspoon Lawry's Seasoned Salt
> 1/2 teaspoon Lawry's Seasoned Pepper
> 1 bottle (12 ounces) Lawry's Classic San Francisco
>   Salad Dressing with Romano Cheese

In resealable plastic bag, combine yellowtail fillet and Herb & Garlic Marinade with Lemon Juice; seal bag. Marinate in refrigerator 1 hour. Remove fish from marinade. Grill fish over medium-high heat 5 minutes each side or until fish just begins to flake; set aside. In large bowl, place lettuce and toss with 4 ounces Classic San Francisco Dressing with Romano Cheese. Arrange remaining vegetables, egg and fish on top of lettuce. Sprinkle with Seasoned Salt, Seasoned Pepper and remaining Classic San Francisco Dressing with Romano Cheese.

Makes 6 servings

Prep time: 20 minutes   Marinate time: 1 hour
Cook time: 10 minutes

Yellowtail Fajitas

Fish fajitas are popular, and for good reason — they're delicious!

2 tablespoons vegetable oil

1 green bell pepper, cut in thin strips

1 onion, thinly sliced

1 pound yellowtail fillets, cut in thin strips

1 package (1.27 ounces) Lawry's Fajitas Spices
   & Seasonings

1/4 cup water

1 medium tomato, cut in thin wedges

Flour tortillas

In large skillet, heat 1 tablespoon oil over medium-high heat. Add green bell pepper and onion; sauté 3 minutes or until tender. Remove from skillet. In same skillet, heat remaining oil over medium-high heat. Add yellowtail, stirring frequently 5 minutes. Add Fajitas Spices & Seasonings and water. Bring to a boil; reduce heat and simmer, uncovered, 3 minutes. Add green bell pepper, onion and tomato; heat through. Spoon into warmed flour tortillas.

Makes 4 servings

Prep time: 15 minutes
Cook time: 12 minutes

Yellowtail with
Fresh Pineapple Salsa

A Mexican fruit salsa adds piquant spice and vibrant color to barbecued fish.

1 cup plus 2 tablespoons Lawry's Hawaiian Marinade
    with Tropical Fruit Juices, divided
1 1/2 pounds yellowtail, cut in 4 1-inch-thick steaks
1 cup fresh pineapple, cut in 1/2-inch pieces, well
    drained
1/4 cup red onion, chopped
2 tablespoons red bell pepper, chopped
1 tablespoon cilantro, chopped
1 tablespoon minced jalapeño chile, seeded

In resealable plastic bag, combine 1 cup Hawaiian Marinade with Tropical Fruit Juices and fish; seal bag. Marinate in refrigerator 30 minutes or up to several hours. In small bowl, lightly mix 2 tablespoons Hawaiian Marinade, pineapple, onion, cilantro, red bell pepper and jalapeño chile. Let pineapple salsa stand at room temperature up to 1 hour. Grill fish over medium-high heat, 5 to 6 minutes each side, or until fish just begins to flake. To serve, spoon salsa over cooked fish.

Makes 4 servings
HINT: 1 can (8 ounces) pineapple chunks, cut in 1/2-inch pieces, well drained, may be substituted for fresh pineapple if desired.

Prep time: 20 minutes   Marinate time: 30 minutes
Cook time: 12 minutes

Butters,
Sauces
& Salsas

Cajun Rémoulade Sauce

This sauce delivers a Cajun kick to complement fish cakes or grilled fish.

1 cup celery, chopped

1 cup green onions, sliced

1/2 cup mayonnaise

1/2 cup parsley

1/3 cup horseradish sauce

1/4 cup whole ground mustard

1/4 cup ketchup

1/4 cup Worcestershire sauce

2 tablespoons Dijon mustard

2 tablespoons red wine vinegar

1 tablespoon paprika

2 teaspoons Lawry's Garlic Powder with Parsley

1 teaspoon Lawry's Seasoned Salt

In food processor or by hand, combine all ingredients; blend well. This sauce may be prepared a day ahead.

Makes 2 cups

Prep time: 15 minutes

Cocktail Sauce

This recipe is a must in every cook's collection.

1/2 cup chili sauce
1/2 cup ketchup
1 tablespoon Worcestershire sauce
1 tablespoon horseradish sauce
1 teaspoon lemon juice
1/2 teaspoon dry mustard
1/2 teaspoon Lawry's Seasoned Salt
1/2 teaspoon Lawry's Seasoned Pepper

In medium bowl, combine all ingredients. Blend well.

Makes 1 cup

Prep time: 10 minutes

Creole Butter Sauce

A delicate sauce especially good with grilled trout.

1 cup butter
2 teaspoons Lawry's Seasoned Salt
2 teaspoons dried thyme
1 teaspoon Lawry's Garlic Powder with Parsley
1 bay leaf, finely crumbled
4 green onions, sliced in 1-inch pieces
1/4 cup chopped yellow bell pepper
1/4 cup dry white wine
1 tablespoon lemon juice

In small heavy saucepan, melt butter over low heat. Add remaining ingredients except wine and lemon juice; simmer 5 minutes, stirring often. Add wine and lemon juice; cook 2 minutes. Purée in blender until smooth, about 30 to 45 seconds.

Makes 1 1/2 cups

Prep time: 10 minutes
Cook time: 10 minutes

Cucumber Sauce

A light sauce with a bit of tang makes a great partnership with fish.

> 1 large English cucumber, peeled
> 1/2 cup mayonnaise
> 1/2 cup sour cream
> 1/4 cup chopped fresh dill
> 1/4 cup chopped fresh chives
> 1 1/2 teaspoons Dijon mustard
> 1 1/2 teaspoons lemon juice
> 1/2 teaspoon Lawry's Seasoned Salt
> 1/4 teaspoon Lawry's Lemon Pepper

In food processor, purée cucumber; do not over-process. Add remaining ingredients. Process until ingredients are just blended.

Makes 3 cups

Prep time: 20 minutes

Dill Sauce with
White Wine Vinaigrette

Fresh dill is a must for this delightful sauce.

1 cup Lawry's Classic White Wine Vinaigrette Dressing
   with Chardonnay
1/2 cup sugar
1/2 cup mayonnaise
1/4 cup snipped fresh dill
2 tablespoons white wine vinegar
1 tablespoon Dijon mustard
2 tablespoons vegetable oil

In small bowl, combine Classic White Wine Vinaigrette with
Chardonnay, sugar, mayonnaise, dill, white wine vinegar and
Dijon mustard. Add oil slowly, beating with wire whisk.

Makes 2 cups

Prep time: 10 minutes

Fresh Avocado Mango Pineapple Salsa

Tropical fruit salsa adds a wonderful blend of flavor and color to grilled fish.

1 1/2 cups diced avocado

1 cup diced pineapple

1 cup diced mango

1/4 cup diced red bell pepper

2 tablespoons cilantro, finely chopped

1 teaspoon Lawry's Citrus Grill Marinade
    with Orange Juice

1 teaspoon Lawry's Garlic Salt

1 teaspoon lime juice

1/8 teaspoon cumin

1/8 teaspoon cayenne pepper

In medium bowl, combine all ingredients; blend well. Cover and chill 30 minutes.

Makes about 3 cups

HINT: If mangos are unavailable, papayas may be substituted.

Prep time: 15 minutes
Chill time: 30 minutes

Lawry's Easy Fish Coating

This tasty coating couldn't be easier. The recipe coats 4 fish to 8 fillets, depending on their size.

> 2 eggs
> 2 tablespoons milk
> 1/2 cup flour
> 1/2 cup potato flakes
> 2 teaspoons Lawry's Lemon Pepper
> 1 1/2 teaspoons Lawry's Seasoned Salt
> 1 1/2 pounds fish fillets
> Vegetable oil for frying

In small bowl, beat eggs and milk together. In shallow dish, combine flour, potato flakes, Lemon Pepper and Seasoned Salt. Pat fish dry. Dip each fish fillet first in egg mixture, then dredge in flour mixture. In skillet, heat oil over medium-high heat until hot. Fry fish 1 to 2 minutes on each side, until golden brown and crispy, or until fish just begins to flake.

Makes 4 to 8 servings

Prep time: 20 minutes
Cook time: 4 minutes

Lemon Pepper and Caper Butter

Lemon and capers are a tangy combo that's a great complement to fish.

1/2 cup (1 stick) butter, at room temperature

2 tablespoons capers, well drained and slightly chopped

1 tablespoon freshly squeezed lemon juice

1 1/2 teaspoons Lawry's Lemon Pepper

In small bowl, combine all ingredients; blend until thoroughly mixed. Adjust seasonings to taste. Spoon butter mixture down the center of a large piece of plastic wrap, waxed paper or aluminum foil; roll it up to shape a 6-inch log. Twist ends and refrigerate until firm, at least 2 hours or up to 2 days. When needed, unwrap butter and cut into slices with warm knife. Serve over grilled or baked fish.

Makes 1/2 cup butter

HINT: Can be frozen up to 1 month.

Prep time: 10 minutes
Chill time: 2 hours

Lemon Pepper Tartar Sauce

A simple sauce for fish burgers or grilled fish.

1/3 cup mayonnaise
2 tablespoons capers, finely chopped
1/2 teaspoon Lawry's Lemon Pepper

In small bowl, combine ingredients; blend well. Refrigerate.

Makes 1/2 cup

Prep time: 5 minutes

Red Pepper Sauce

A colorful condiment for baked or grilled fish.

2 red bell peppers, roasted, skin and seeds removed

3/4 cup fresh bread crumbs

1/4 cup fish stock OR chicken stock

2 tablespoons olive oil

1 teaspoon Lawry's Garlic Powder with Parsley

1 teaspoon Lawry's Seasoned Salt

1/2 teaspoon Lawry's Seasoned Pepper

In medium bowl, combine all ingredients; blend or grind to a thick paste. This may be done in food processor.

Makes about 2 cups

Prep time: 20 minutes

Spicy Cocktail Sauce

Just the right dipping sauce for seafood.

1 cup ketchup
2 tablespoons white horseradish sauce
1 tablespoon lemon juice
1 tablespoon Worcestershire sauce
1 tablespoon tarragon vinegar
1/8 teaspoon Lawry's Seasoned Salt
1/8 teaspoon Lawry's Garlic Powder with Parsley
2 drops hot pepper sauce

In medium bowl, combine all ingredients; blend well.

Makes about 1 cup

Prep time: 7 minutes

Tartar Sauce

A tangy sauce that is excellent on fish.

1 cup mayonnaise
2 tablespoons chopped gerkins
1 tablespoon capers with 1 teaspoon juice
4 teaspoons Dijon mustard
4 teaspoons chopped fresh parsley
1 teaspoon chopped fresh tarragon
1 teaspoon Lawry's Garlic Powder with Parsley
1 teaspoon lemon juice
3/4 teaspoon dried chervil
1/2 teaspoon anchovy paste (optional)

In medium bowl, combine all ingredients; blend well. Best when made a day in advance and refrigerated overnight.

Makes about 1 1/2 cups

HINT: Parsley may be substituted for tarragon if desired.

Prep time: 10 minutes
Chill time: 24 hours

Summer Vegetable and Fruit Salsa

Salsa = sauce. This salsa equals great taste!

1 cup diced red bell pepper
1 cup diced tomato
1 cup diced nectarine
1/3 cup diced red onion
1 tablespoon chopped cilantro
1/2 teaspoon Lawry's Garlic Salt
1/2 teaspoon lime juice
1/8 teaspoon ground cumin

In medium bowl, combine all ingredients; blend well. Let stand 30 minutes before serving, if desired.

Makes about 3 cups

Prep Time: 15 minutes
Standing Time: 30 minutes

Fish Substitutions

Pacific barracuda ...   *bonito, bluefin tuna, catfish*

Pacific bonito ....   *yellowfin tuna, flounder, catfish*

Calico bass ....   *white seabass, red snapper, spotted trout*

Catfish ....   *amberjack, dorado, yellowtail*

Halibut ....   *grouper, red snapper, monkfish*

King salmon ....   *trout, swordfish, amberjack*

Mako shark ....   *swordfish, yellowfin tuna, grouper*

Rainbow trout ....   *king salmon, swordfish, rock cod*

Red snapper ....   *rock cod, white seabass, calico bass*

Sand bass ....   *spotted trout, calico bass, catfish*

Sculpin ....   *spotted trout, red fish, rock cod*

Sheephead ....   *rock cod, white seabass, calico bass*

White seabass ....   *calico bass, rock cod, red fish*

Yellowfin tuna ....   *swordfish, shark, amberjack*

Yellowtail ....   *amberjack, dorado, halibut*

Order Form

I want to order _____ copies of *A Fisherman's Cookbook* @ $9.^{95} plus $3.^{00} *S & H.*
(Make check payable to Corbin Publishing)

Name _____

Address _____

City _____ State _____ Zip _____

Country _____

I want to order _____ copies of *A Fisherman's Cookbook* @ $9.^{95} plus $3.^{00} *S & H.*
(Make check payable to Corbin Publishing)

Name _____

Address _____

City _____ State _____ Zip _____

Country _____

Send form and check to:

Corbin Publishing • P.O. Box 90 • Montebello, CA 90640

website:
www.sport-fishing.com

e-mail:
sptfishing@aol.com

NOTES

NOTES

NOTES

NOTES